Bond

No Nonsense

English

8–9 years

Contents

Handwriting practice

Central pull-out pages

Copy this piece of writing on the lines underneath.

The trolls ran forward. They carried torches in their hands and sharp axes. They gnashed their teeth and howled at the moon. Firelight shone on their helmets. The castle lay dark and silent. No sound came from the walls. An owl hooted far away in the night.

The trolls ran forward. They carried torches in their hands and sharp axes They gnashed their teeth and howled at opy this poem on the lines underneath.

From underneath the kitchen table,
Sliding fast across the floor,
saw the jelly slithering outwards,
Travelling fast towards the door.
gave a shout, I turned to run,
nearly made it out the gate,
Up behind I heard a squelching,
Slipped and fell – it was too late!

Syllables

Separating words into **syllables** (a **beat** or sound) makes them easier to read and to spell. In two-syllable words that have **double consonants** in the middle, the double consonants are split between the syllables:

kit / ten   pol / len   ot / ter

Each syllable has a vowel in it and the double consonants follow a **short vowe** sound.

1. **Underline the double consonants, then split these words into two syllables.**

   a common _com_ / _mon_   b sorry _sor_ / _ry_

   c traffic _traf_ / _fic_   d shopping _shop_ / _ping_

2. **Join the correct syllable pairs, then write the completed words.**

   a swal ⟍ ma   _swallow_   d car low   _carrot_

   b sud — low   _sudden_   e hol ting   _hollow_

   c com den   _comma_   f get rot   _getting_

3. **Write the two-syllable words with double consonants that match these definitions.**

   a A cushion for your head when you sleep. _pillow_

   b A young dog. _puppy_

   c A sport played on a court with racquets and balls. _tennis_

   d The season that follows spring. _summer_

4. **Write two, two-syllable words with double consonants to rhyme with each of the words below.**

   a mummy _tummy_ _bunny_

   b butter _clutter_ _shutter_

0	Tough	OK	Got it! 15

Total

/15

Homophones

Homo means **same** and **phone** means **sound**.
Homophones are words that **sound the same** but they are **spelt differently** and have **different meanings**.

sum / some   **mail / male**   **road / rode**

QUICK TIP!
The **context** of a sentence will help you find the right homophone.

1. **Join the pairs of homophones.**

meat   our   week   cereal   bored   hole   hare

whole   serial   hour   meet   hair   weak   board

2. **Think of a homophone for each of these common words.**

a leek _____   **b** eye _____   **c** brake _____

d night _____   **e** steel _____   **f** piece _____

g aloud _____   **h** pour _____   **i** wood _____

3. **Choose the correct homophone to complete these sentences.**

a Yasmin bought a _____new_____ (knew / new) _____ (pear / pair) of shoes.

b Jack _____blew_____ (blew / blue) his _____ (knows / nose).

c Jen went _____pale_____ (pail / pale) when she _____ (heard / herd) the story.

d They _____ (tide / tied) a firm _____knot_____ (knot / not) to secure the boat.

e We went to Hastings to _____ (sea / see) the _____. (sea / see)

f He _____threw_____ (through / threw) the ball _____ (through /threw) the window.

g He told a _____ (tail / tale) about a fox's bushy _____. (tail / tale)

h We all turned to _____ (stair / stare) at the black cat on the _____. (stair / stare)

0			18
Tough	OK	Got it!	

Total

/18

Regular verb endings

Verbs (**doing words**) tell us **what has happened** (past tense), **what is happening** (present tense) and **what will happen** (future tense).

Lots of verbs have **regular endings**.

verb	past tense	present tense	future tense
walk	I walk**ed**	I am walk**ing** *or* I walk	I will walk
play	I play**ed**	I am play**ing** *or* I play	I will play
watch	I watch**ed**	I am watch**ing** *or* I watch	I will watch

The verb must agree with the subject of the sentence: **I** walk / **he** walk**s**

1. **Add the correct present tense ending, where needed, to these verbs.**

    a   He like___s___ scrabble but he prefer___s___ playing football.

    b   They are walk___ing___ across the field.

    c   I am talk___ing___ to my mum on the telephone.

2. **Add the correct past tense ending, where needed, to these verbs.**

    a   Jack roll___ed___ the spare tyre onto the drive and lift___ed___ it into the car boot.

    b   They open___ed___ the door, the cat jump___ed___ out and climb___ed___ the tree.

    c   The dog chase___ed___ the rabbit until it disappear___ed___ into a deep hole.

3. **Add the correct verb ending, where needed.**

    a   Julie remind___ed___ her to bring her book when they talk___ed___ yesterday.

    b   "Can you help_____ me?" ask___ed___ the old man. "My friend borrow___ed___ my radio and now I am look___ing___ for her."

    c   He was talk___ing___ to his mum and she ask___ed___ him if he was plan___ing___ to do his homework before dinner.

0				9	Total
	Tough	OK	Got it!		9

Irregular verb endings

Some verbs endings are **irregular**. They have different forms in the present and past tense:

Present: I can **swim**.   Past: I **swam** in the pool.

Some irregular forms follow **rules** that can help you learn the changes:

1. Verbs ending in **ow** (present) change to **ew** (past): bl**ow** / bl**ew**

2. Verbs ending in **ell** (present) change to **old** (past): t**ell** / t**old**

Other irregular verbs do not follow any rules and just have to be learned:

think / **thought**   eat / **ate**   have / **had**

Match the past and present tense words.

grow	knew	creep	kept	sing	rang
throw	grew	keep	wept	ring	drank
know	threw	weep	crept	drink	sang

2. **Write the past tense of these verbs.**

a find __found__   b speak _____   c shake _____

d tear __tore__   e sell _____   f wind __winded__

3. **Complete the sentences with the past tense of the verbs in brackets.**

a The boy __felt__ his way down the dark passageway. (feel)

b I __bought__ a new game for my computer in the sale. (buy)

c He __drew__ a picture of his family and gave it to his Mum. (draw)

d When he washed the jumper he __shrank__ it by mistake. (shrink)

e The bread __rose__ in the oven while it was cooking. (rise)

f "I __taught__ Year 4 last term," replied the teacher. (teach)

g She _____ her pocket money on a new dress. (spend)

		Total
0		14	
Tough	OK	Got it!	/14

Suffixes

Suffixes are letter strings that are added to the **end** of a word. When a suffix is added, the **meaning** of the new word is **different** to the meaning of the root word.

friend + **ship** = friendship   child + **hood** = childhood

fit + **ness** = fitness   fulfil + **ment** = fulfilment

Simply add these suffixes, unless the word ends in **y**. For these words, change the **y** to an **i** and then add the suffix.

happ**y** + ness / happiness

1. **Choose a suffix to change the words below into new words.**

   a manage ___ment___   **b** false _ment_   **c** move _ment_

   d member _ence_   **e** state _ment_   **f** priest _ment_

   g owner _ment_   **h** father _ment_   **i** partner _ment_

2. **Make new words from these root words by adding the suffix 'ness'.**

   a mad ___madness___   **b** lovely _lovelyness_   **c** sad _sadness_

   d nasty _nastiness_   **e** silly _silliness_   **f** greedy _greediness_

   g kind _kindness_   **h** tidy _tidiness_   **i** fair _fairness_

3. **Complete each sentence with a word ending in 'ship', 'hood' or 'ment'.**

   a Sunil lost his pencil so Mrs Taylor gave him a _replacement_ _newment_.

   b Pete was really excited as his team had won the _chievement_ _achivement_.

   c We know all of the families who live in our _neigh_ _neibourhor_ _neibourha_.

   d We should all take care of nature and the _environment_.

   e To become a qualified plumber, Tim had to complete an _appriment_.

0   Tough   OK   Got it!   21

Total

21

8

More suffixes

Some suffixes can change some **nouns** (n) and **adjectives** (adj) into **verbs** (v).

light (n) + **en** = lighten (v)

If a root word ends in an **e** or a **y**, they must be removed before adding the suffix.

not**e** (n) + **ify** = notify (v)   apolog**y** (n) + **ise** = apologise (v)

The spelling of some root words must change before a suffix can be added.

medicine (n) + **ate** = medic**ate** (v)

. **Change these words into verbs by adding either the suffix 'en' or 'ate'.**

a pollen _____ **b** alien _____ **c** deep _____

d wide _____ **e** fix _____ **f** dark _____

. **Change these words into verbs by adding either the suffix 'ise' or 'ify'.**

a solid _ify_____ **b** character _____ **c** class _____

d final _ise_____ **e** simple _ify_____ **f** horror _____

. **Remove the suffixes to change these verbs into nouns or adjectives.**

✴ **a** elasticate _____ **b** awaken _____ **c** purify _____

d strengthen _____ **e** standardise _____ **f** liquidate _____

4. **Add a suffix to the correct word below to complete each sentence.**

~~active~~   justice   ~~straight~~   ~~gold~~

a Ranjit had to _justify_____ his answer using evidence from the text.

b The magic goose lay _____ eggs.

c You had to push the red button to _____ the robot.

d Mary could not decide whether to curl or _____ her hair.

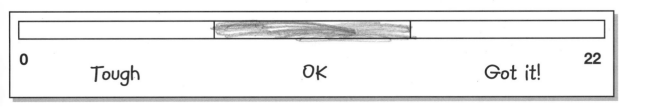

0			22
	Tough	OK	Got it!

Total

22

9

Verbs

> Verbs are **doing** words – they tell you **what is happening** in a sentence. A sentence does not make sense without a verb.
>
> Verbs must **agree** with the **singular** or **plural** subject of a sentence.
>
> **1.** Singular means just **one** person or thing is doing something: **I / you / he / she / i**
>
> **2.** Plural means **more than one: we / you / they**

1. **Complete each sentence with the correct present tense form of the verb in brackets.**

   a Mark _____ football in the park after school. (play)

   b I _____ watching TV but Sally _____ it. (like / hate)

   c When he _____ to work, Dad _____ his bags. (go / carry)

   d All the children _____ songs in assembly. (sing)

2. **Choose the correct form of the past tense to complete each sentence.**

   a Jason _____ back home because he _____ his books. (forget / run)

   b When Asher _____, her Mum _____. (swim / cheer)

   c They _____ down the road and _____ the bus. (catch / go)

   d Raj _____ when he _____ over. (yell / fall)

3. **Group the verb forms under the correct headings in the table.**   *(3 marks)*

   am marrying   are speaking   is crying   are marrying   am crying

   is speaking   are crying   am speaking   is marrying

	To cry	To marry	To speak
I	am crying	am marrying	am speaking
He / She	is crying	is marrying	is speaking
They / You	are crying	are marrying	are speaking

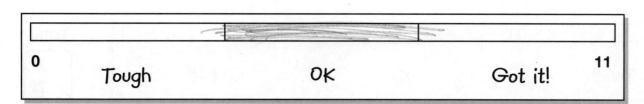

| 0 | Tough | OK | Got it! | 11 |

Total

/11

Verb tenses

> The **tense** of a verb tells you **when** something happened.
> **Present tense** – something that is **happening now**:
>   I **eat** my lunch now.
> **Past tense** – something that has **already happened**:
>   I **ate** my lunch yesterday.
> **Future tense** – something that **will happen**:
>   I **will eat** my lunch tomorrow.
> The most common way to refer to something in the future is to add **will** or **shall** before the verb.

. **Write the correct forms of these verbs for the subjects shown.** *(4 marks)*

Verb	Past tense	Present tense	Future tense
to touch	I _touched_	I	I
to go	you	you	you
to speak	she _spoke_	she _is speaking_	she
to fly	they _flew_	they	they

Write the past tense forms of the verb to sleep.

a I _____   **b** he _____   **c** she _____

d we _____   **e** you _____   **f** they _____

3. **Use the correct form and tense of the verbs in brackets to complete the sentences.**

a Dad _____ the flowerbed in the garden yesterday. (to dig)

b Tomorrow we _____ to Dover. (to drive)

c Gran _____ a pink scarf for me now. (to knit)

d We _____ the circus last Saturday. (to see)

e Next Sunday I _____ nine years old. (to be)

f I _____ for a swim after school yesterday. (to go)

g It is lovely and warm today because the sun _____. (to shine)

Tough	OK	Got it!

0   17

Total

17

Powerful verbs

> Using **powerful verbs** can make your writing more interesting and sentences will give **more effective descriptions**.
>
> He **ran** down the road and **asked** for help.
>
> The common verbs in bold can be replaced to make the sentence more descriptive:
>
> He **sprinted** down the road and **begged** for help.

QUICK TIP!
Use a thesaurus to help find more powerful verbs.

1. **Think of four powerful verbs that mean the same as like.** *(4 mark:*

   _____ _____ _____ _____

2. **Match the pairs of common and more powerful verbs.**

   said   ate   fly   leave   took

   depart   snatched   gobbled   replied   soar

3. **Complete the sentences using other powerful verbs that mean the same as walked**

   a The old lady _____ down the hall in her slippers.

   b Slowly they _____ along the road enjoying the sunshine.

   c The girl _____ into the room clutching her bleeding hand.

   d They _____ along, mile after mile, to reach the town.

4. **Use the correct past tense form of a powerful verb to replace each common verb in brackets.**

   a Don _____ to catch up with Asim. (to run)

   b Sara _____ to Liz so no one could hear her. (to speak)

   c The plate slipped off the table and _____ on the stone floor. (to break)

   d The boy _____ through the bushes and saw a badger. (to look)

   e They _____ up the cliff face to escape the oncoming tide. (to climb)

0		14
Tough	OK	Got it!

Total

/14

Adverbs

Adverbs give more information about verbs. Many adverbs describe **how** something happens.
Adverbs answering the question 'How?' usually end in **ly**.
  She spoke **slowly**.   She spoke **loudly**.
But not all of them!
  fast   well

QUICK TIP!
Remember the rules for adding suffixes.

. **Turn these words into 'how' adverbs by adding the suffix 'ly'.**

a quick _____*quickly*_____   b thick _____   c strange _____

d curious _____   e secret _____   f speedy _____

g normal _____   h angry _____   i quiet _____

2. **Underline the 'how' adverbs.**   (5 marks)

She easily got the top marks in the exam. Carefully she put away her exam paper and walked home quickly. As she got inside, her dog started to bark noisily. "You always bark at me," she said, "You never bark at Mum!" She wondered if she should try opening the door more quietly tomorrow!

3. **Choose different 'how' adverbs to complete these pairs of sentences.**

a I play my trumpet very _____.

   I play my trumpet very _____.

b Please will you write _____.

   Please will you write _____.

c He was dressed incredibly _____.

   He was dressed incredibly _____.

			Total
0 Tough	OK	Got it! 16	16

More adverbs

As well as describing **how** something happens, adverbs can also describe **when** **where** or **how often** something happens.

Where did the dog play?	The dog played **outside**.
When did Joe arrive?	Joe arrived **late**.
How often does she dance?	She dances **regularly**.

1. **Underline the adverbs and write which group they belong to – how, when, where or how often.**

   a The snow floated gently to the ground. _____

   b He was glad to be inside. _____

   c Tommy rarely did as he was told. _____

   d I went to bed early. _____

Sometimes adverbs are written with other words to make a word group. These are called **adverbial phrases**.
   She played her radio **all the time**.   Put your bag **over there**.

2. **Choose one of these adverbial phrases to complete these sentences.**

more than enough	not surprisingly	as quickly as
over there	over and over	all the time

   a She finished her work _____ possible.

   b Their dog barked _____.

   c "There's _____ food on your plate."

   d "Put your bag _____ next to mine, Abdul."

   e She practised the exercise _____ again to get it right.

   f _____, the game was over after the fourth goal.

0			10	Total
Tough	OK	Got it!		/10

Phrases and clauses Lesson 12

A **phrase** is a group of words that refers to something or someone.
   some water   a tall man
A **clause** is a group of words that tells you what someone/something did or what happened to them/it.
   she drank some water   she was thirsty
A **clause** contains a verb but phrases don't.

. **Write whether these are phrases or clauses.**

a the tiny cottage   _____

b they went for a walk _____

c a cold wind blew   _____

d a cup of tea   _____

e I closed my eyes   _____

f a miserable person _____

Sentences are made up of one or more clauses.
Sometimes a clause makes sense on its own but sometimes it needs another clause to make sense.
   I hurried home   as soon as I had finished
       ↑   ↑
    clause 1   clause 2
Clause 2 only makes sense when it is written in a sentence with clause 1.
I hurried home as soon as I had finished.

2. **Tick the clauses that make sense on their own.**

a every day no matter how tired he is feeling _____

b my dad stays up late _____

c I got up early before the sun had risen _____

d to take the dog for a walk _____

0		10
Tough	OK	Got it!

Total
/10

15

Speech marks and commas

> **Speech marks** show when **someone is speaking**.
>
> When a sentence of speech is **interrupted**, **commas** are used to show the interruption and the second part begins with a **small letter** (not a capital letter).
>
> "If you want my opinion," said Ade, "those trousers are too long for you."
>
> If a **new sentence** starts after the interruption, the new sentence follows a **full stop** and starts with a **capital letter**.
>
> "Where is my bag?" said Mike. "It has disappeared."

1. **Put speech marks round the spoken words in these sentences.**

   a It's your turn to kick the ball, said Mike. You'll never score a goal from there!

   b Is that right? she asked Mrs Smith. I think that answer looks wrong.

   c Don't be greedy! said Shelley to her little sister. That chocolate is mine!

   d Is that who I think it is? laughed Gran. My goodness you've grown!

   e If you like, said Susie, we can go swimming later.

   f Can you really wrestle sharks, Dad? asked Ben. Aren't they dangerous?

2. **Write speech marks and commas in these sentences where needed.**

   a I can't come   cried Sally   because it's Katie's birthday party.

   b Please be quiet   ordered her teacher   and get on with your work!

   c Look! I know I should've told you before   he yelled   but it's not my fault!

   d Well she said it certainly looks like someone has broken in.

   e I promised I'd help you she yelled angrily and I will so leave me alone!

   f Tomorrow said Zac we are going to the cinema.

0		12
Tough	OK	Got it!

Total

/12

Commas

> Individual **commas** are used to separate a **list** of things in a sentence. If there are **more than two** items in the list, we usually put **and** before the last item:
>
>   She bought beans, carrots, lettuce **and** tomatoes.
>
> Sometimes it is not necessary to use **and** before the last adjective:
>
>   She brushed her long, flowing, dark hair.
>
> **Pairs of commas** mark **extra** (non-essential) **information** in sentences:
>
>   Mrs Jones, our teacher, was away today.

. **Separate the items in the lists using commas and 'and' where necessary.**

a On a cold   clear   night you can see the stars easily.

b Sarah bought some apples   pears   grapes   bananas yesterday.

c Den scuffed along the dry   silky   golden sand in his bare feet.

2. **Create sentences with extra information separated by commas.**

Miss Mann,	our head teacher,	can run very fast.
Lucy,	my friend,	is learning to fly an aeroplane.
Mr Adams,	the television presenter,	enjoys playing the piano.

a _____

b _____

c _____

3. **Use commas to separate the extra information from the rest of each sentence.**

a Judy my mother and Tom my father went to visit Grandad.

b Since my visit to the dentist Ms Kanas my toothache has gone away.

c We took Wendy my best friend to the big retail park on Saturday.

Tough	OK	Got it!

0   9

Total

9

Classic fiction

Read this passage based on *Gulliver's Travels*, then answer the questions.
Gulliver's boat was overturned by a large wave and sank out at sea. He swam to the shore but was worn out by the time he reached it so lay down to sleep.

When he awoke he could not move. He was pinned to the ground with fine rope and nails. On his chest stood a little man, no more than six inches high, and around him were forty more little people. Gulliver was so surprised that he shouted "Oh!" in a loud voice and all the people ran away.

Gulliver started to laugh loudly. A little man in a red and gold pointed hat and a red cloak with gold stitching on it peeped out. Gulliver smiled at him and whispered, "Hello, who are you?"

"I'm the Emperor of Lilliput," the little man stated proudly. "Who are you?"

"My name is Gulliver. Where am I?"

"Why, in Lilliput of course!" was the Emperor's reply.

1. **Who is the main character? Circle the correct answer.**

    a The Emperor   **b** Gulliver   **c** Lilliput

2. **Did he sleep before or after the boat sank?** _____

3. **Why couldn't he move when he woke up? Circle the correct answer.**

    a A man was standing on him.

    b A crowd of people were holding onto him.

    c Ropes were holding him down.

    d He was too tired.

4. **Who did he see first?** _____

5. **What is the key characteristic of the people of Lilliput?**

    _____

6. **Was Gulliver a good swimmer? Give a reason for your answer.**

    _____

. **Why did Gulliver laugh loudly?**

_____

. **Do the Lilliputians have nervous characters? Give a reason for your answer.**

_____

. **How do you know the Emperor is important, before he introduces himself?**

_____

10. **Put these events in chronological order (the order in which they happened).**

   a The Lilliputians ran away from Gulliver.

   b The Lilliputians tied Gulliver up with ropes.

   c Gulliver escaped from his sinking boat.

   d The Emperor told Gulliver where he was.

   e Gulliver slept on the shore.

   f Gulliver woke up.

   1 _Gulliver_ _____

   2 _____

   3 _____

   4 _____

   5 _____

   6 _____

0   Tough   OK   Got it!   15

Total

15

Fact and opinion

Information that is based on **truth** and which can be **proved** is called **fact**.

What someone **thinks** or **believes** about something is called **opinion**.

It is important to be able to **tell the difference** between fact and opinion when reading and collecting information on a topic.

Read the extract below and then answer the questions.

Tiger population near extinction?

Environmentalists today launched a campaign to save the Bengal tiger, as there are concerns that it is now facing extinction.

Bengal tigers are found across India and live in forests, dense areas of long grass and riverbanks. They usually live alone but occasionally small groups of tigers have been spotted travelling together – assumed to be as a result of the mating season or when cubs are still too young to survive by themselves.

Adults can weigh between 350 and 500 pounds, have large eyes with excellent vision and also have excellent hearing. They have large canine teeth and padded paws with long, sharp claws. Some people wear necklaces made from the claws, as they believe the claws will protect them from evil spirits. Their whiskers are long and thick and it is a belief in Malaysia that they can be used to make deadly poisons. The tigers also have white spots on their ears and it has been suggested that a mother may use these spots to keep track of her cubs in dark forests and during the night.

Bengal tigers have been hunted heavily by man and are now labelled as an endangered species. Some people estimate that around 4000 tigers still exist in India, but others say that less than 3000 now live in the wild.

1. **What is an environmentalist? Circle the correct answer.**

    a someone who looks after tigers

    b someone who researches wild animals

    c someone concerned with protecting our natural environment

2. **Where do Bengal tigers live? Circle the correct answer.**

    a China   **b** India   **c** Malaysia

How heavy are the tigers? Circle the correct answer.

a under 350 pounds   **b** over 500 pounds

c between 350 and 500 pounds

. **What do Malaysians believe can be used as an ingredient for poison? Circle the correct answer.**

a a tiger's claws   **b** a tiger's tail   **c** a tiger's whiskers

. **Which short phrase in the 1st paragraph indicates that something is opinion?**

_____

. **Which three short phrases in the 3rd paragraph indicate that something is opinion?**   (*3 marks*)

_____

_____

_____

7. **Are these statements fact or opinion, according to the article?**

a Mother tigers rely on white ear spots to find their cubs at night. _____

b Tigers are carnivores and have huge teeth to bite their prey. _____

c Tigers travel in groups during mating season. _____

d Tigers have long whiskers and padded paws. _____

e Tigers' claws should be worn to ward off evil spirits. _____

f Man has hunted tigers and the species is now in danger. _____

g There are 4000 tigers living in India. _____

h Tigers live in forests and along riverbanks. _____

0   16

Tough   OK   Got it!

Total

16

How am I doing?

1. **Split these words into syllables.**

   a hippo _____ / _____   **b** rubber _____ / _____   **c** batter _____ / _____

   d coffee _____ / _____   **e** willow _____ / _____   **f** swimming _____ / _____

2. **Join the pairs of homophones.**

   male   bear   pale   knight   flower   heir

   flour   night   mail   air   bare   pail

3. **Complete the sentences with the correct past tense forms of the verbs in brackets.**

   a My dad _____ tomatoes in the greenhouse last summer. (grow)

   b Tom _____ down the hallway and out of the front door. (creep)

   c Amrita _____ the ball and the batsman was out of the game. (catch)

4. **Add the correct suffix: ship, hood, ment, ness, en, ify, ise or ly to complete these words.**

   a boy _____   **b** excite _____   **c** workman _____

   d drama _____   **e** gold _____   **f** happy _____

   g different _____   **h** simple _____

5. **Use the correct verb form and tense to complete these sentences.**

   a We _____ Grandma tomorrow. (to visit)

   b I _____ a ham sandwich for lunch yesterday. (to eat)

   c Look! The sun _____ and it's a lovely day. (to shine)

6. **Use powerful verbs to replace the common verbs in brackets.**

   a "I _____ cheese and pickle sandwiches – they're my favourite!" (to like)

   b Charlie _____ as he thought the joke was really funny. (to laugh)

   c "Please, please, please can we go Mum?" _____ Sanjay. (to ask)

Turn these words into adverbs by adding the ly suffix.

a swift _____   **b** gentle _____   **c** heavy _____

d extreme _____   **e** silent _____   **f** clumsy _____

Choose one of these adverbial phrases to complete these sentences.

as quickly as   over there   very slowly   all the time

a She ate dinner _____ possible, as she was late for her piano lesson.

b He played his music _____ when he was at home.

c "Scott, stand _____ next to Susan and wait for your turn."

d The old man crossed the road _____.

9. **Write whether these are phrases or clauses.**

a the black, white and brown cat _____

b the cat jumped _____

10. **Rewrite these sentences, using the correct punctuation.**

a Although it was cold Dad and I went for a run round the park

_____

b Good morning Mrs Fisher said the doctor What seems to be the problem

_____

c I need to buy carrots leeks broccoli a pound of potatoes thought Mary

_____

d My sister Emily is younger than I am but my brother Carl is older

_____

			Total
Tough	OK	Got it!	

0   40

/40

Using a dictionary

A **dictionary** is arranged in **alphabetical order**. If words begin with the **same** letter, they are arranged in order by the **following** letters. For example:

that then thin thorn thumb – these words are arranged by their **3rd** letters.

straw stream strip stroke strum – these words are arranged by their **4th** letters

1. **Write each word in the correct place in the alphabetical lists below.**

   a casserole cafeteria capital

   cabbage _____ calendar _____ caravan _____

   b bright brick bring

   _____ bridge _____ brilliant _____ brisk

   c getaway geese geography general

   _____ gem _____ _____ gerbil _____

2. **Put these words in alphabetical order.**

   a marshmallow marble market marry

   _____ _____ _____ _____

   b prickle priest print price prince

   _____ _____ _____ _____ _____

   c label learn ladder least lady

   _____ _____ _____ _____ _____

0			6
Tough	OK	Got it!	

Total

6

Plurals

SpellingLesson 18

To form **plurals** for words ending with the letters **ff** or **ve**, just add **s**.

   one pu**ff** / two pu**ffs**   one glo**ve** / two glo**ves**

To form plurals for words ending with the letters **f** or **fe**, change the **f** to a **v** and then add **es**.

   one wol**f** / two wol**ves**   one kni**fe** / two kni**ves**

Not all words that end in **f** follow this rule, some just add **s**.

   one roo**f** / two roo**fs**

. Write the plural form of these words.

a dive _____   **b** wave _____   **c** cliff _____

d curve _____   **e** sniff _____   **f** cuff _____

g dove _____   **h** sieve _____   **i** ruff _____

2. Write the singular form of these words.

a loaves _____   **b** shelves _____   **c** calves _____

d wives _____   **e** thieves _____   **f** halves _____

g scarves _____   **h** selves _____   **i** lives _____

3. Group these words under the correct heading for their plural endings.

surf   loaf

sheriff   belief

hoof   elf

leaf   chef

reef   thief

bluff   cove

ves	s

0			19
Tough	OK	Got it!	

Total

19

25

Word endings: ight and ite

Many words share **common endings**. Learning these letter strings can help you spell unknown words.

One common ending is the **ight** sound. Most words with this sound are nouns and use the letter string **ight**, for example **light**.

Some words that have the same **ight** sound are spelt differently – they use the letter string **ite**, for example **site**.

1. **Complete these words using the correct ending.**

   a br _____   **b** k _____   **c** fl _____   **d** wr _____

2. **Tick the words spelt correctly and write the correct spellings of the incorrectly spelt words.**

   a spight _____   **b** fite _____   **c** excite _____   **d** plite _____

   e fright _____   **f** tight _____   **g** delite _____   **h** nite _____

3. **Complete these sentences using an 'ight' or 'ite' word.**

   a The names of 25 kn_____s were written on the Round Table.

   b "I went to the concert last n_____ and it was brilliant!"

   c John got nine out of ten questions r_____ in the test.

   d "What a s_____! Get into the bath now and wash off all that mud!"

   e The magician pulled a large, wh_____ rabbit out of his hat.

   f Ranjit had just taken a b_____ out of his sandwich when the phone rang.

   g "If you're good, I m_____ let you stay up a bit later this evening."

   h Sally was qu_____ pleased with the results of her shopping trip.

   i The teacher used a coloured pen to highl_____ the key words in the text.

   j "My favourite TV programme is on ton_____ – I can't wait!"

0 Tough   OK   Got it! 22

Total / 22

Prefixes

Spelling | Lesson 20

Look at the meanings and examples of these four prefixes.

ad means **to, towards**: **ad**just

af means **tending towards**: **af**fix

al means **all**: **al**together

a means **on** or **in**: **a**ground

. **Choose one prefix to complete all the words for these definitions.**

a To come towards: _____vance **b** To be next to something: _____jacent

c It describes a verb: _____verb **d** The process of adding: _____dition

e It describes a noun: _____jective **f** To recommend or inform: _____vise

2. **Complete these words using one of the prefixes.**

a ___ ways **b** ___ sleep **c** ___ most **d** ___ firm **e** ___ way

f ___ fable **g** ___ one **h** ___ vent **i** ___ join **j** ___ stride

3. **Complete the sentences by adding a prefix to each word in brackets.**

a Mum told me to do my homework but I had _____ done it. (ready)

b They chased each other _____ the park. (round)

c Pat started her homework _____ she had only just got home. (though)

d People had difficulty telling the twins _____. (part)

e Dad says that people who are _____ have lots of money. (fluent)

f When the fire brigade arrived, the house was _____. (blaze)

0		22
Tough	OK	Got it!

Total

/22

27

Gender

Many nouns tell you about the **gender** of a person or animal – if it is **male** (m) or **female** (f).

Most nouns have **different** words for male and female terms.

Lord (m) / **Lady** (f)   **boy** (m) / **girl** (f)   **stallion** (m) / **mare** (f)

Sometimes the suffix **ess** is added to a male (masculine) word to create the female (feminine) version. lion / lion**ess**

1. **Match the male and female animal pairs.**

   fox   drake   ram   bull   buck   tiger   gander

   ewe   tigress   cow   goose   doe   duck   vixen

2. **Underline the masculine words and circle the feminine words below.**

   mother   duke   princess   stewardess   host   duchess   heir

   countess   steward   heiress   father   count   hostess   prince

3. **Complete these sentences using the opposite gender of the words in bold.**

   a The **king** and _____ sat on their thrones in the Great Hall.

   b They gave their **nephew** and _____ two birthday presents each.

   c In the play the _____ and **heroine** were very young.

   d When they got married the vicar declared them _____ and **wife**.

   e The farmer bought another **hen** and a _____.

   f **Uncle** George and _____ Betsy are coming for dinner tomorrow.

   g We were served by a **waiter** and a _____ in the restaurant.

   h "Look! The **cob** and _____ are teaching their cygnets to swim!"

   i My favourite **actor** and _____ are in this film.

0			11
Tough	OK	Got it!	

Total

/11

Making adjectives

> The suffixes **ful / able / ing / less** change **verbs** (v) and **nouns** (n) into **adjectives** (adj).
>
> wash (v) + **able** = wash**able** (adj)   shock (n) + **ing** = shock**ing** (adj)

. **Choose a suffix to change these nouns and verbs into adjectives.**

> **QUICK TIP!**
> Some nouns and verbs can be changed by more than one suffix.

a help _____

b live _____

c respect _____

d smile _____

e shine _____

f thank _____

g bear _____

h love _____

i enjoy _____

j hope _____

> **QUICK TIP!**
> Remember the rules when adding suffixes.
> • change **y** to **i**
> • delete the **e**

2. **Complete the sentences by adding the correct suffix to the words in brackets.**

a He was always on time. He was very _____. (rely)

b The sky was dark and the _____ rain soon fell. (pour)

c He was rude and completely _____. (charm)

d She was so selfish, she was utterly _____. (thought)

e They couldn't help showing off, they were so _____. (boast)

f Her exam results were very good; they were truly _____. (remark)

g She was jealous of her brother and rather _____. (resent)

h It wasn't the tool for the job; it was really _____. (use)

i The lovely curtains were a _____ shade of pink. (taste)

0 Tough	OK	Got it! 19

Total

19

Comparatives and superlatives

Adjectives give you **extra** details about nouns and pronouns: The **red** balloon.

Adjectives also **compare** things: Clare is **tall**, John is **taller**, but Ravi is the **tallest**.

These three types of comparing adjectives are called:
* **simple form**   Maths is **easy**.
* **comparative form**   French is eas**ier**.
* **superlative form**   English is the eas**iest** of all.

Look how the **endings** change for each form.

1. Write the comparative and superlative forms of these adjectives.   *(4 marks*

Simple	Comparative	Superlative
short	shorter	
windy		
thin		
sunny		

2. Complete the sentences with the correct forms of the adjectives in brackets.

a Yesterday it was _____ but today it is even _____. (cold)

b The flight to America was the _____ she had ever taken. (long)

c My _____ day was when Dad brought home the puppy. (happy)

d Sally was _____ but her brother was _____. (smart)

e It was the _____ thing she had ever done. (hard)

f The hare was the _____ and ran much _____ than the tortoise. (fast)

g The last dive was the _____ of all. (scary)

h He was the _____ boy in the class. (noisy)

0			12
Tough	OK	Got it!	

Total

/12

Similes

Grammar | Lesson 24

Similes (pronounced sim-ill-ees) create a picture in the reader's mind by **comparing** one thing with another, usually to exaggerate.

The giant was **as big as a house**.   The horse was **as white as snow**.

. **Underline the similes in these sentences.**

a His hands were as cold as ice.

b We crept up behind him as quiet as mice.

c He was as hungry as a wolf by dinner time.

d The temperature in the kitchen was as hot as the sun.

e Her look was as hard as nails.

2. **Join up the similes.**

a As brave as   an ox   **b** As wise as   a cucumber

c As strong as   coal   **d** As white as   an owl

e As black as   a lion   **f** As cool as   a sheet

3. **Complete each simile with the most appropriate word.**

silk   bat   button   lightning   bee   bone   pancake   toast

a Sam had so much to do she was as busy as a _____.

b The tyre was as flat as a _____.

c Without her glasses, she was as blind as a _____.

d The horse was as quick as _____.

e He was so thirsty – his throat was as dry as a _____.

f With the fire on, they were as warm as _____.

g The performance went as smooth as _____.

h Having had a good night's sleep, she was as bright as a _____.

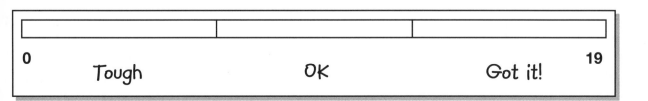

			Total
0 Tough	OK	Got it! 19	19

31

Powerful adjectives

Adjectives help the reader to picture what the writer is describing.
Some adjectives are **more powerful** than others.

It was a **blazing hot** summer day   builds a very different picture from

It was a **warm bright** summer day.

The first sentence uses **more powerful** adjectives than the second one.

1. **Circle the most powerful adjective of each pair.**

   a frozen / cool   **b** nice / enchanting   **c** ravenous / hungry

2. **Choose from the adjectives below to complete these sentences.**

   freezing   expensive   scorching   tart   gigantic   sweet   tiny   affordable

   a The North Pole is _____ but the Equator is _____.

   b Lemon meringue pie tastes _____ but chocolate cake is _____.

   c A giant is _____ but a dwarf is _____.

   d Gold jewellery is _____ but costume jewellery is _____.

3. **Put these adjectives in order, going from one extreme to the other.**

   a chilly   warm   tepid

   hot   _____   _____   _____   cold

   b moist   soaked   soggy

   dry   _____   _____   _____   saturated

   c plain   pretty   fair

   ugly   _____   _____   _____   beautiful

			Total
0 Tough	OK	Got it! 10	/10

32

Bond

No Nonsense
English

8–9 years

Parents' notes

What your child will learn from this book

Bond No Nonsense will help your child to understand and become more confident at English. This book features the main English objectives covered by your child's class teacher during the school year. It provides clear, straightforward teaching and learning of the essentials in a rigorous, step-by-step way.

This book begins with some **handwriting practice**. Encourage your child to complete this carefully and to continue writing neatly throughout the book.

The four types of lessons provided are:
Spelling – these cover spelling rules and strategies.
Grammar – these cover word types and sentence construction.
Punctuation – these cover punctuation marks and their rules.
Comprehension – these cover reading different types of text and comprehension questions.

How you can help

Following a few simple guidelines will ensure that your child gets the best from this book:
- Explain that the book will help your child become confident in their English work.
- If your child has difficulty reading the text on the page or understanding a question, do provide help.
- Encourage your child to complete all the exercises in a lesson. You can mark the work using this answer section. Your child can record their own impressions of the work using the 'How did I do?' feature.

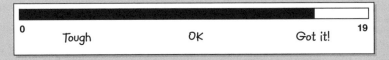

0			19
	Tough	OK	Got it!

- The 'How am I doing?' sections provide a further review of progress.

Bond No Nonsense 8–9 years Answers

① Syllables p4
1 a com / mon   b sor / ry   c traf / fic   d shop / ping
2 b sudden   c comma   d carrot
   e hollow   f getting
3 a pillow   b puppy   c tennis   d summer
4 Possible answers include:
   a tummy / yummy   b flutter / mutter

② Homphones p5
1 meat / meet   our / hour   week / weak   cereal / serial
   bored / board   hole / whole   hare / hair
2 a leak   b I   c break   d knight
   e steal   f peace   g allowed   h poor
   i would
3 a new / pair   b blew / nose   c pale / heard
   d tied / knot   e see / sea   f threw / through
   g tale / tail   h stare / stair

③ Regular verb endings p6
1 a likes / prefers   b walking
   c talking
2 a rolled / lifted   b opened / jumped / climbed
   c chased / disappeared
3 a reminded / talked
   b help / asked / borrowed / looking
   c talking / asked / planning

④ Irregular verb endings p7
1 throw / threw know / knew creep / crept keep / kept
   weep / wept sing / sang ring / rang drink / drank
2 a found   b spoke   c shook
   d tore   e sold   f wound
3 a felt   b bought   c drew   d shrank
   e rose   f taught   g spent

⑤ Suffixes p8
1 b falsehood   c movement   d membership
   e statement   f priesthood   g ownership
   h fatherhood   i partnership
2 b loveliness   c sadness   d nastiness
   e silliness   f greediness   g kindness
   h tidiness   i fairness
3 a replacement   b championship   c neighbourhood
   d environment   e apprenticeship

⑥ More suffixes p9
1 a pollenate   b alienate   c deepen   d widen
   e fixate   f darken
2 a solidify   b characterise   c classify   d finalise
   e simplify   f horrify
3 a elastic   b awake   c pure   d strength
   e standard   f liquid
4 a justify   b golden   c activate   d straighten

⑦ Verbs p10
1 a plays   b like / hates   c goes / carries   d sing
2 a ran / forgot   b swam / cheered
   c went / caught   d yelled / fell
3 I am crying; he/she is crying; they/you are crying
   I am marrying; he/she is marrying; they/you are marrying
   I am speaking; he/she is speaking; they/you are speaking

⑧ Verb tenses p11
1 I touched; I touch/I am touching; I will touch/I am going to touch
   you went; you go/you are going; you will go/you are going to go
   she spoke; she speaks/she is speaking; she will speak/she is going
   to speak they flew; they fly/they are flying; they will fly/they are
   going to fly
2 a I slept   b he slept   c she slept
   d we slept   e you slept   f they slept
3 a dug   b will drive / are going to drive   c is knitting
   d saw   e will be / am going to be   f went
   g is shining

⑨ Powerful verbs p12
1 Possible answers include: adore / love / enjoy / admire
2 said / replied ate / gobbled fly / soar leave / depart took / snatched
3 Possible answers include:
   a shuffled   b ambled   c burst   d trudged
4 Possible answers include:
   a raced   b whispered   c smashed   d peered
   e scrambled

⑩ Adverbs p13
1 b thickly   c strangely   d curiously   e secretly
   f speedily   g normally   h angrily   i quietly
2 easily / Carefully / quickly / noisily / quietly
3 Answers will vary

⑪ More adverbs p14
1 a gently (how)   b inside (where)   c rarely (how often)
   d early (when)
2 a as quickly as   b all the time   c more than enough
   d over there   e over and over   f Not surprisingly

⑫ Phrases and clauses p15
1 a phrase   b clause   c clause
   d phrase   e clause   f phrase
2 b ✓   c ✓

⑬ Speech marks and commas p16
1 a "It's your turn to kick the ball," said Mike. "You'll never score a
      goal from there!"
   b "Is that right?" she asked Mrs Smith. "I think that answer looks
      wrong."
   c "Don't be greedy!" said Shelley to her little sister. "That chocolate
      is mine!"
   d "Is that who I think it is?" laughed Gran. "My goodness you've grown!"
   e "If you like," said Susie, "we can go swimming later."
   f "Can you really wrestle sharks, Dad?" asked Ben. "Aren't they
      dangerous?"
2 a "I can't come," cried Sally, "because it's Katie's birthday party."
   b "Please be quiet," ordered her teacher, "and get on with your work!"
   c "Look! I know I should've told you before," he yelled, "but it's not my
      fault!"
   d "Well," she said, "it certainly looks like someone has broken in."
   e "I promised I'd help you," she yelled angrily, "and I will, so leave me
      alone!"
   f "Tomorrow," said Zac, "we are going to the cinema."

⑭ Commas p17
1 a On a cold, clear night you can see the stars easily.
   b Sarah bought some apples, pears, grapes and bananas yesterday.
   c Den scuffed along the dry, silky, golden sand in his bare feet.
2 Possible answers include:
   a Miss Mann, our head teacher, enjoys playing the piano.
   b Lucy, my friend, can run very fast.
   c Mr Adams, the television presenter, is learning to fly an aeroplane.
3 a Judy, my mother, and Tom, my father, went to visit Grandad.
   b Since my visit to the dentist, Ms Kanas, my toothache has gone
      away.
   c We took Wendy, my best friend, to the big retail park on Saturday.

⑮ Classic fiction p18
1 b
2 He slept after the boat sank.
3 c
4 He first saw a little man standing on his chest.
5 They are all very small people.
6 Yes, because he swam to the shore when his boat sank out at sea.
7 He laughed when he saw all the little people run away.
8 Yes, because they all ran away when Gulliver first spoke.
9 He is described as wearing a red and gold hat and cloak which
   implies that he is a man of importance.
10 c e b f a d

⑯ Fact and opinion p20
1 c   2 b   3 c   4 c
5 there are concerns
6 they believe / it is a belief / it has been suggested
7 a opinion   b fact   c opinion   d fact
   e opinion   f fact   g opinion   h fact

How am I doing? p22
1 a hip / po   b rub / ber   c bat / ter   d cof / fee
   e wil / low   f swim / ming
2 male / mail   bear / bare   pale / pail   knight / night
   flower / flour   heir / air
3 a grew   b crept   c caught
4 a boyhood   b excitement   c workmanship   d dramatise
   e golden   f happiness   g differently   h simplify
5 a will visit / are going to visit   b ate   c is shining
6 Possible answers include:
   a love   b giggled   c pleaded

a swiftly   b gently   c heavily   d extremely
e silently   f clumsily
a as quickly as   b all the time   c over there   d very slowly
a phrase   b clause
a Although it was cold, Dad and I went for a run round the park.
b "Good morning, Mrs Fisher," said the doctor, "What seems to be the problem?"
c "I need to buy carrots, leeks, broccoli and a pound of potatoes," thought Mary.
d My sister, Emily, is younger than I am but my brother, Carl, is older.

7 Using a dictionary p24

a cabbage / cafeteria / calendar / capital / caravan / casserole
b brick / bridge / bright / brilliant / bring / brisk
c geese / gem / general / geography / gerbil / getaway
a marble / market / marry / marshmallow
b price / prickle / priest / prince / print
c label / ladder / lady / learn / least

8 Plurals p25

a dives   b waves   c cliffs   d curves   e sniffs
f cuffs   g doves   h sieves   i ruffs
a loaf   b shelf   c calf   d wife   e thief
f half   g scarf   h self   i life
ves: hoof / leaf / elf / loaf / thief / cove
s: surf / sheriff / bluff / reef / belief / chef

9 Word endings: ight and ite p26

a bright   b kite   c flight   d write
a spite   b fight   c ✓   d plight
e ✓   f ✓   g delight   h night
a knights   b night   c right   d sight
e white   f bite   g might   h quite
i highlight   j tonight

10 Prefixes p27

a advance   b adjacent   c adverb   d addition
e adjective   f advise
a always   b asleep   c almost   d affirm
e away   f affable   g alone   h advent
i adjoin   j astride
a already   b around   c although   d apart
e affluent   f ablaze

21 Gender p28

dog / vixen   drake / duck   ram / ewe   bull / cow
buck / doe   tiger / tigress   gander / goose
Masc.: duke / host / heir / steward / father / count / prince
Fem.: mother / princess / stewardess / duchess / countess / heiress / hostess
a queen   b niece   c hero   d husband
e cockerel   f Aunt / Auntie   g waitress   h pen   i actress

22 Making adjectives p29

1 a helpful / helpless   b livable or liveable / living
c respectable / respectful   d smiling
e shining   f thankful / thankless
g bearable / bearing   h lovable / loving / loveless
i enjoyable   j hopeful / hopeless
2 a reliable   b pouring   c charmless   d thoughtless
e boastful   f remarkable   g resentful   h useless
i tasteful

23 Comparatives and superlatives p30

1 short / shorter / shortest   windy / windier / windiest
thin / thinner / thinnest   sunny / sunnier / sunniest
2 a cold / colder   b longest   c happiest   d smart / smarter
e hardest   f fastest / faster   g scariest   h noisiest

24 Similies p31

1 a as cold as ice   b as quiet as mice
c as hungry as a wolf   d as hot as the sun
e as hard as nails
2 a As brave as a lion   b As strong as an ox
c As black as coal   d As wise as an owl
e As white as a sheet   f As cool as a cucumber
3 a bee   b pancake   c bat   d lightning
e bone   f toast   g silk   h button

25 Powerful adjectives p32

1 a frozen   b enchanting   c ravenous
2 a freezing / scorching   b tart / sweet
c gigantic / tiny   d expensive / affordable
3 a hot / warm / tepid / chilly / cold
b dry / moist / soggy / soaked / saturated
c ugly / plain / fair / pretty / beautiful

26 Making more adjectives p33

1 a childish   b foolish   c newish
d reddish   e sevenish
2 a greatest   b older / oldest   c greener
d tidier   e warmer / warmest   f sharpest

27 Adverbs and adjectives p34

1 a almost   b extremely   c highly   d too
2 a incredibly (adv) / affectionate (adj)
b completely (adv) / wonderful (adj)
c really (adv) / colourful (adj)
d particularly (adv) / sour (adj)
e quite (adv) / difficult (adj)
3 Possible answers include:
a extremely   b really   c so   d just   e thoroughly

28 Possessives 1 p35

1 a Joe's toy   b Merri's skirt   c the baby's pram
d the dog's lead
2 a The pen belonging to my dad   b The purse belonging to my mum
c The boots belonging to the boy   d The fur of the cat
e The tail of the fox
3 a Paul's   b spectator's   c team's   d boy's
e Sasha's   f Paul's

29 Possessives 2 p36

1 a man's   b boy's   c horse's   d Imran's / Sonny's
2 a tigers'   b tables'   c girls'   d televisions'
e members'
3 a The fur coats of my dogs   b The pages of the book
c The pages of the books   d The skins of the potatoes
e The bowl belonging to the cat

30 Its and it's p37

1 a its   b its   c it's   d It's   e its / It's   f it's / its
2 "Its 9.30am," / "Its getting late …" / One of it's legs / finish it's
programme / Its such / stalls its got / around it's neck

31 Expressive language p38

1 b   2 c   3 c
4 a very distant land
5 magicians / wizards / goblins / dwarfs
6 all sparkling with light
7 brilliant diamonds
8 crazy / untidy
9 crammed / peeling / crumbling / sagged / bulged
10 'bulged, like bumps'
11 Individual answers.

32 Explanatory texts p40

1 c   2 d   3 a
4 No, in the last sentence it states: 'to start the continuous water recycling process again.'
5 The passage says that air can be warm when it is heated by the sun and also cold when it rises.
6 formal style / present tense
7 Any four of: vapour / evaporation / atmosphere / condense / condensation / precipitation
8 a labelled diagram
9 numbered paragraphs and technical language
10 There is no separate conclusion but the text does draw to a conclusion as the final sentence brings the cycle back to the first stage detailed in the first paragraph. You would not expect any more information to be given.

How am I doing? p42

1 band / banner / barbecue / bargain / barn
2 a earmuffs   b captives   c rashes   d explosives
e wives   f reefs
3 a kite   b fight   c slight   d delight
e spite
4 a apart   b affirm   c address   d around
e also   f admire   g adjoin   h awake
5 billy / nanny   baron / baroness   viscount / viscountess
sir / lady   emperor / empress   ram / ewe
6 a joyful   b skilful   c capable   d singing
7 jollier / jolliest larger / largest cheaper / cheapest sharper / sharpest
8 a as dry as a bone   b as deaf as a post
c as sharp as a razor   d as sweet as a honey
e as straight as an arrow   f as slippery as an eel
9 filthy / dirty / grubby / dusty / clean / spotless
10 a saddest   b babyish   c livelier
11 a very   b most   c quite
12 a chairs'   b brother's   c girls'   d dog's
13 a It's / its   b it's / It's   c its / its

㉝ Letter strings: wa and wo p44

1 **a** awake (3) **b** watch (1) **c** swamp (1)
   d wallet (1) **e** wall (2)
2 **a** woman (2) **b** work (1) **c** worm (1)
   d wool (2) **e** world (1)
3 **a** sword **b** beware **c** two **d** worse
   e worry **f** awoke

㉞ Letter strings: ough and ou p45

1 oh: dough / boulder / although ow: drought / hour / ground
   oo: route / youth / coupon uh: country / thorough / double
   aw: court / bought / fought
2 **a** pour / trough **b** your / wound / could
   c Would / you / four / counters

㉟ Common roots p46

1 dictare: diction / dictionary / dictate / dicatator
   presse: depress / pressure / express / compress
   esventer: invention / advent / preventative / ventilator
   specere: spectator / inspection / spectrum / spectacles
2 **a** telescope **b** horoscope **c** microscope **d** stethoscope
3 Possible answers include:
   a telephone / saxophone
   b autograph / biography
   c aquamarine / aquarium
   d octopus / October

㊱ Vowel suffixes p47

1 ive: relative / narrative / expensive / active / massive
   ic: terrific / allergic / photographic / artistic / acidic
   ist: balloonist / machinist / novelist / conservationist / extremist
2 **a** allergic **b** artistic **c** photographic **d** expensive
   e massive **f** novelist **g** relative **h** machinist

㊲ Compound words p48

1 **a** blackboard **b** raspberry **c** tablecloth **d** handbag
   e homework **f** outside **g** blackbird **h** goodnight
   i moonlight **j** cloakroom
2 Possible answers include:
   a bedroom / bedclothes / bedtime
   b housework / household / housebound
   c anyone / anytime / anything
   d sunshine / sunflower / sunbathe
   e something / someone / somewhere
3 **a** newspaper **b** grasshopper / flowerbed
   c strawberry / milkshake **d** landlord

㊳ Diminutives p49

1 **a** piglet **b** bullock **c** gosling
   d duckling **e** eaglet **f** kitten
2 **a** minimal **b** minimum **c** microphone
   d microchip **e** miniature **f** microscope
3 **a** Anthony / Tony **b** Daniel / Dan **c** Benjamin / Ben
   d Elizabeth / Liz **e** James / Jim **f** Timothy / Tim
   g Nicholas / Nick **h** Victoria / Vicky
4 **a** brunette **b** anklet **c** dumpling

㊴ Verb endings p50

1 you were / are / will
   he, she or it was / is / will
   we were / are / will
   they were / are / will
2 **a** I will walk **b** he will pack **c** we will run
   d they will swim
3 **a** left **b** drove **c** will move
   d will finish **e** will be **f** arrived

㊵ Comparative endings p51

1 **a** safer / safest **b** bigger / biggest **c** prettier / prettiest
2 **a** most **b** more **c** more / most
3 **a** much more / dearest **b** much more **c** more
   d most / much

㊶ Plural nouns p52

1 **a** calendars **b** coaches **c** kisses **d** dominoes
   e foxes **f** holidays **g** photos **h** cries
   i accidents **j** glasses **k** gases **l** watches
2 **a** cacti **b** oases **c** antennae **d** gateaux
   e fungi **f** formulae
3 **a** species **b** sheep / deer **c** salmon / trout **d** series

㊷ Connectives p53

1 **a** if/then **b** although **c** so
   d due to **e** but

2 **a** in fact **b** therefore **c** unless
   d On the other hand **e** however **f** as a result
   g nevertheless **h** since **i** whereas

㊸ Different kinds of sentences p54

1 **a** question **b** positive statement **c** question
   d order **e** negative statement
2 **a** Come with me!
   b Sit down!
   c Never do that again!
   d Leave!
3 **a** I'm not staying with Neha tonight.
   b We are not going shopping now.
   c I can't do my homework later.

㊹ Colons and semicolons p55

1 **a** first line: Solomon Grundy. **b** as follows: two …
   c aloud: To …
2 **a** the sun; it … **b** bike; it …
   c cucumber; four fresh river salmon; and …
3 **a** words: "Friends … **b** dinner; Mum …
   c features: air-conditioning; all electric windows; two airbags in the
   front; a CD player; and …

㊺ Hyphens p56

1 **a** Bourton-on-the-Water **b** three-year-old / half-time
   c decision-making / four-wheel
2 **a** father-in-law / sister-in-law **b** second-hand / three-piece-suit
   c Sixty-three / low-key **d** clean-shaven / self-confidence
   e re-cover / re-place **f** passer-by / break-in

㊻ Dashes p57

1 **a** opportunity – and **b** park – everyone
   c events – see the attached note – the **d** the map – the map
2 **a** girls – Ellen and Adhira – were **b** night – very
   c visit – do **d** go – but
   e the diary – the diary **f** brother – he

㊼ Poetry p58

1 at the field's edge
2 They were too nervous to go into the field.
3 Their ears flickered to and fro.
4 dogs and men
5 daintily
6 spring
7 glossy as the new grass / soft as wool / brown
8 He was down-wind and hidden by the oaks.
9 They could not smell him.
10 **a** like swimmers too nervous to go in / glossy as the new grass, soft
   as wool / moving like water
   b dancers practising their steps / a stream of brown
11 He wants to stroke them.

㊽ Persuasive writing p60

1 **c**
2 **c**
3 Dropped food or scraps, food packaging, sweet wrappers, empty
   bottles and cans, waste paper, chewing gum
4 Someone who leaves litter around.
5 Lazy Litter Louts / health hazard / ticking time / spread serious
6 a ticking time bomb
7 Litter is a health hazard
8 Individual answers.
9 discarded / drop / toss / dump
10 The word 'litter' is repeated to give maximum emphasis and to act
   as a constant reminder to the reader as to the topic of the article.
11 It's a health hazard. You could be fined or taken to court.

How am I doing? p62

1 **a** twosome **b** wasp **c** worry **d** water
   e sword **f** swarm
2 uh: tough / rough / enough ow: hour / shout / bough
   aw: bought / your / nought oo: through / you / route
   oh: boulder / though / mould
3 Possible answers include:
   decade / decimal / December
4 **a** relative **b** narrative **c** allergic **d** terrorist
   e novelist **f** photographic
5 **a** shoebox **b** playground **c** clubhouse
6 **a** ducklings **b** miniature **c** owlet **d** kitchenette
7 **a** faster / quicker **b** more / cheapest **c** most
8 **a** spades **b** fungi **c** libraries **d** socks
9 **a** however **b** if … then **c** no matter how
10 **a** statement **b** question **c** order
11 **a** safe: two … **b** words: "A rose …
   c needed: four fresh apples; small green grapes; and …
12 **a** Moreton-in-Marsh **b** amazing – and …
   c ex-teacher / supermarket – and

Making more adjectives

Adjectives which **deepen**, **heighten** or **strengthen** our thoughts and feelings about things, often end with the suffixes **ish**, **er** or **est**.

These sentences compare the intensity of the word **cool**.

It is rather **cool** today. It was a **coolish** day yesterday.

It was **cooler** the day before but the **coolest** day was Sunday.

QUICK TIP!
Remember the rules for adding suffixes: **double consonants** after **short vowels** and change **y** into **i.**

Choose an adjective and add the ish suffix to complete the sentences.

new   child   seven   fool   red

a Despite his age, at times his behaviour was extremely _____.

b I don't know who felt more _____ when I found out about their lie, Sara or Nikki.

c It was not an old table, in fact it was _____.

d Her hair was a _____ brown colour.

e "Can you meet me at about _____? I'm running late."

Add 'ish', 'er' or 'est' to the words in brackets to complete the sentences.

a He was said to be the _____ footballer of all time. (great)

b I think my uncle is _____ than my aunt but Gran is the _____. (old)

c The grass is always _____ on the other side of the fence. (green)

d Mum says that my sister's room is _____ than mine. (tidy)

e My room is _____ than Jo's, but Simon's is the _____. (warm)

f The bread knife is the _____ in the drawer so we don't touch it. (sharp)

Tough	OK	Got it!

11

Total

11

Adverbs and adjectives

Adverbs are often used with **adjectives** to express how much or how little (the **degree** to which) the adjective applies.

scarcely   nearly   just

The most frequently used adverb of degree is **very**: It was a **very** hot day.

1. **Underline the adverbs in these sentences.**

   a "Hurry up! Dinner is almost ready."

   b She was extremely lucky not to be hurt when she fell off her bicycle.

   c There was a highly peculiar smell coming from the kitchen.

   d "I can't do it, it is too difficult!"

2. **Underline the adverbs and circle the adjectives in these sentences.**

   a Cats are incredibly affectionate animals.

   b She had a completely wonderful day.

   c It was a really colourful piece of work.

   d The tangerines that Mum bought were particularly sour.

   e It was quite a difficult sum and she couldn't work it out.

3. **Choose suitable adverbs to complete these sentences.**

   a My maths homework was _____ difficult today.

   b It was such a _____ funny film it made me roar with laughter.

   c It's _____ annoying when she phones in the middle of dinner!

   d We had _____ sat down when the doorbell rang.

   e Abby was _____ confused and had to ask the teacher for help.

Tough	OK	Got it!

0   14

Total

14

34

Possessives 1

Apostrophes are used to show **possession** (to whom something belongs):

It is Sally's book.

To check where to put the apostrophe, turn the sentence round like this:

Sally's book = the book **belonging to** Sally.

The apostrophe must go after Sally because the book belongs to Sally. It is Sally's book.

. **Rewrite these phrases using an apostrophe to show possession.**

a A toy belonging to Joe _____

b A skirt belonging to Merri _____

c The pram of the baby _____

d The lead for the dog _____

2. **Write these phrases out in full so that an apostrophe isn't needed.**

a My dad's pen _____

b My mum's purse _____

c The boy's boots _____

d The cat's fur _____

e The fox's tail _____

3. **Write in the missing 's in these sentences.**

a Paul team won the match.

b The spectator seat was soaking wet.

c Habib scored the team first goal.

d The boy face was filthy.

e Alison gave Jody Sasha address.

f That isn't mine it's Paul .

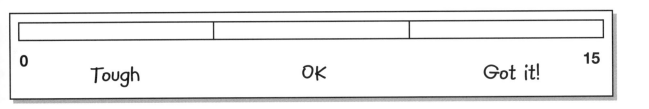

0
Tough
OK
Got it!
15

Total

/ 15

35

Possessives 2

> Apostrophes are used to show **singular** and **plural** forms of possession.
>
> In singular forms of possession, the apostrophe is written **before the s**:
>
> The girl**'s** doll – the doll belonging to **one** girl.
>
> In plural forms of possession, the apostrophe is written **after the s**:
>
> The girl**s'** doll – the doll belongs to **more than one** girl.

1. **Put the 's in the correct place for a singular possessive noun.**

    a The old _____ walking stick was broken. (man)

    b It was that _____ fault. (boy)

    c The _____ stable needed mucking out. (horse)

    d "Is that _____ or _____ ?" (Imran / Sonny)

2. **Write the plural forms of the nouns in brackets, using apostrophes to show possession.**

    a The _____ roars in the still night were frightening. (tiger)

    b "Both those _____ legs are wobbling." (table)

    c "Our _____ singing voices are delightful." (girl)

    d All the _____ signals were poor due to the bad weather. (television)

    e That's the _____ entrance, we have to go round to the front." (member)

3. **Rewrite these phrases without using an apostrophe.**

    a My dogs' fur coats _____

    b The book's pages _____

    c The books' pages _____

    d The potatoes' skins _____

    e The cat's bowl _____

0			14
Tough	OK	Got it!	

Total

14

Its and it's

The words **it's** and **its** have very different meanings.

it's is a **contraction** meaning **it is** or **it has**.
It's cold out there!

its means something **belonging** to it.
The cat sat in **its** basket.

To check if the correct word has been used:

- read **it is** or **it has** instead of **it's**. If neither make sense, use **its**.

1. Choose it's or its to complete these sentences.

a The fish swam round _____ tank.

b I knew which bicycle I wanted but I wasn't sure about _____ colour.

c I'm afraid _____ going to be a very long journey.

d " _____ now or never!" he said.

e The cat licked _____ paws. _____ time for his dinner," she thought.

f The horse cannot jump as _____ hurt _____ legs.

2. Read this passage and circle each mistake when its or it's are incorrectly used.

(7 marks)

"Mum, what time is it?" called Toby.

"Its 9.30am," replied Mum.

"Its getting late, when are we leaving?" asked Toby, as he started jumping up and down in his chair.

"Be careful Toby! That chair is unsteady. One of it's legs is loose," said Mum. "It's OK, calm down. I am waiting for the washing machine to finish it's programme, so I can hang the washing out on the line. Its such a warm day, that it should be dry by the time we get back."

They were soon in the car and Mum drove them to the park. "What's that?" asked Toby, pointing ahead. "It's a fair," smiled Mum. "Come on, let's go and see what stalls its got!" Mum won Toby a teddy bear which had a bright red scarf around it's neck.

0 Tough	OK	Got it! 13

Total

/13

Expressive language

When authors write about imaginary or fantasy worlds they use **expressive** language to help build pictures of **moods**, **settings** and **characters** in the reader's mind. They create these pictures by using features of language such as **powerful verbs**, **adjectives**, **adverbs** and **similes**.

Read this extract then answer the questions.

It all happened a very long time ago, in a very strange city, in a far away land. The city was built on the banks of a river. When the morning sun was shining, it shone on hundreds of towers and spires and domes, and set them all sparkling with light. They looked like brilliant diamonds, but the buildings beneath them were dark. The streets were narrow and small. The houses were crammed together, at crazy angles, in untidy rows. Their walls were peeling and crumbling, and their roofs sagged. They had lots of little rooms in them that bulged and looked like bumps. It was a strange city, all right – a strange, bent, rather sinister city, and some strange, bent, rather sinister creatures lived there: magicians, wizards, goblins, dwarfs.
The city was ruled by a sinister man, as well, whose name was Horg. You wouldn't have wanted to live in this city. But Franz lived there.

1. **Where has the city been built? Circle the correct answer.**

   a in a strange place   **b** next to a river   **c** in the hills

2. **How many domes and towers are there? Circle the correct answer.**

   a one hundred   **b** one thousand   **c** hundreds

3. **What are the houses like? Circle the correct answer.**

   a light and airy   **b** dark and spacious   **c** dark and tightly packed

4. **What phrase in the first sentence implies that this is a story about an imaginary world?**

   _____

Which four nouns near the end of the passage confirm that this is an imaginary world?

_____

. The first part of the description of the city seems fresh and bright. Which phrase best gives this impression?

_____

. What simile does the author use to describe the brightness of the city?

_____

. Find two adjectives that describe how the houses were crammed together.

_____

_____

9. Which five powerful verbs describe the miserable houses?

_____

_____

_____

10. Find an alliterative phrase that describe the rooms.

_____

_____

11. Does the expressive language give you a vivid picture of the city? Can you explain how?

_____

_____

_____

_____

0		11
Tough	OK	Got it!

Total

/11

Explanatory texts

> The main purpose of an **explanatory text** is to **explain** something. There are man
> types of explanatory texts, such as: **manuals**, **science books** and **history books**
>
> Explanatory texts usually have these features: an **introduction**; **paragraphs** that
> organise the text in sequence; a **summary** or **conclusion**; the use of **technical**
> language; and **diagrams** or **illustrations**.

Read this explanatory text, and then answer the questions.

How does the water cycle work?

1. The heat from the sun gradually dries up some of the water from rivers, lakes, oceans, seas and the land and transforms it into tiny droplets in the air or water vapour. This process is called evaporation.
2. Air rises when it is warmed by the sun. You cannot see air moving but you can sometimes see how it carries things, like smoke from a bonfire, high up into the sky. As warm air rises, it carries the water vapour from the land and the sea up into the atmosphere.
3. The higher the air rises, the cooler it becomes and this eventually causes the water vapour to condense, forming tiny water droplets or ice crystals which we can see in the form of clouds. This process is called condensation.
4. When the droplets become too heavy to remain floating in the air, they fall back down to the land and sea. If the air is warm, the droplets fall as rain but if it is cold the droplets form ice crystals and fall as sleet or snow. This process is called precipitation. Some of this precipitation soaks down into the ground while most flows downhill, joining rivers and streams, and eventually returns to the seas and oceans to start the continuous water recycling process again.

1. **What is this text explaining? Circle the correct answer.**

   a how much water we have   **b** how to make bonfires

   c the water cycle

2. **Where is water found? Circle the correct answer.**

   a rivers and lakes   **b** oceans and seas

   c in the atmosphere   **d** all of these areas

3. **How does water get into the sky? Circle the correct answer.**

   a it turns into water vapour   **b** it is carried by clouds

   c it is taken up by smoke

Does the water cycle only happen once? How do you know?

_____

_____

Is air warm or cold when it rises? How do you know?

_____

_____

What language style and tense is the text written in?

_____

The text introduces some technical terms. Write four of them.   (4 marks)

_____   _____

_____   _____

8. Which key feature of explanatory texts, that would be useful to help understand the water cycle, is missing?

_____

9. Which features does this explanatory text use?

_____

10. Does this text have a conclusion, or do you think there is more information to follow? Why?

_____

_____

_____

_____

0		13
Tough	OK	Got it!

Total

/ 13

1. **Put these words in alphabetical order.**

   barn   barbecue   band   bargain   banner

   _____   _____   _____   _____   _____

2. **Write the plurals of these words.**

   a earmuff _____   **b** captive _____   **c** rash _____

   d explosive _____   **e** wife _____   **f** reef _____

3. **Complete these words with the correct common ending: ight or ite.**

   a k_____   **b** f_____   **c** sl_____   **d** del_____   **e** sp_____

4. **Add the prefixes a, ad, af or al to complete these words.**

   a _____part   **b** _____firm   **c** _____dress   **d** _____round

   e _____so   **f** _____mire   **g** _____join   **h** _____wake

5. **Match the masculine and the feminine nouns.**

   billy   baron   viscount   sir   emperor   ram

   empress   nanny   ewe   baroness   lady   viscountess

6. **Choose a suffix to change these nouns into adjectives: ful, able or ing.**

   a joy _____   **b** skill _____   **c** cap _____   **d** sing _____

7. **Write the comparatives and superlatives for these words.**

Simple	jolly	large	cheap	sharp
Comparative				
Superlative				

Join up the similes.

a as dry as   a post

b as deaf as   a razor

c as sharp as a bone

d as sweet as   an eel

e as straight as honey

f as slippery as an arrow

Put these adjectives in order, going from one extreme to the other.

clean   dirty   grubby   dusty

filthy _____ _____ _____ _____ spotless

0. Choose a suffix ish, er or est to complete the adjectives.

a She spoke in the _____ tone of voice. (sad)

b "Stop being so _____ ! It's time to go." (baby)

c The brown puppy was _____ than the black and white one. (lively)

1. Choose an adverb (quite, very or most) to complete the sentences.

a Mum looked across at me and said, "You're not _____ talkative today."

b "What is the _____ important job of the day?" asked her Dad.

c "Vanilla ice cream is _____ tasty," said James, "but chocolate is my favourite."

12. Put the 's in the correct place for the singular and plural nouns.

a All the _____ legs were loose. (chairs)

b Her _____ toys were all over the floor. (brother)

c The _____ names were Joya and Rachel. (girls)

d That _____ tail is really long and bushy. (dog)

13. Choose it's or its to complete these sentences.

a "_____ his car and _____ exhaust needs replacing."

b "Hi, _____ me. Can I come in? _____ raining out here!"

c The fox caught _____ leg on the fence and had to lick ____ wound clean.

Total

46

Letter strings: wa and wo

The letter string **wa** is pronounced differently in different words.

1. In most words it sounds like **wo**.		**wa**sh	s**wa**t
2. If it is followed by **l** or **r** it sounds like **wor**.		**wa**lk	s**wa**rm
3. In **one syllable** words ending in **e** or **y** it sounds like **way**.	**wa**ve	s**wa**y

---

1. Answer these clues using words containing wa. Write 1, 2 or 3 to show how wa is pronounced in each word.

   a The opposite of asleep. _____ _____

   b You wear it on your wrist and it tells the time. _____ _____

   c A bog or marshy ground. _____ _____

   d Men keep their money in one of these. _____ _____

   e A barrier made of bricks. _____ _____

The letter string **wo** is also pronounced differently in different words.

1. In most words it sounds like **wer**.	**wo**rds
2. If it is followed by another **o** it sounds like it is written **woo**.	**woo**den

---

2. Answer these clues using words containing wo. Write 1 or 2 to show how wo is pronounced in each word.

   a Opposite of better. _____ _____

   b What people do to earn money. _____ _____

   c A creature with no legs that lives in soil. _____ _____

   d Balls of this are used to knit jumpers. _____ _____

   e Another name for the Earth. _____ _____

3. Write the correct spelling of each of these wa and wo words. They do not follow the rules for pronouncing wa and wo.

   a soard _____   **b** bewair _____   **c** too _____

   d wimen _____   **e** wurry _____   **f** awoak _____

0			16	Total
Tough	OK	Got it!		/16

Letter strings: ough and ou

The letter strings **ough** and just **ou** can be pronounced in several different ways.

Sounds like	ough	ou
'oh'	th**ough**	m**ou**ld
'ow'	b**ough**	f**ou**nd
'oo'	thr**ough**	gr**ou**p
'uh'	bor**ough**	y**ou**ng
'aw'	**ough**t	m**ou**rn

. **Group these words together by their pronunciation.**   *(15 marks)*

dough   country   drought   thorough   route   court   hour   boulder
bought   youth   double   fought   coupon   although   ground

oh	ow	oo	uh	aw

2. **Complete the sentences with ough or ou words that are pronounced like the sounds in brackets.**

a The farmer is going to p_____r the food into the pigs' t_____gh. ('aw' / 'off')

b "Show me y_____ r w_____nd, it c_____ld be infected." ('aw' / 'oo' / 'uh')

c "W_____ld y_____ lend me f_____r c_____nters Asif?" ('uh' / 'oo' / 'aw' / 'ow')

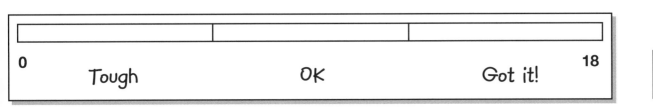

0	Tough	OK	Got it! 18

Total

/18

Common roots

QUICK TIP!
Use a dictionary
if you need help

Many of our words are built on **common roots**.
Lots of everyday words have come to us from other languages over hundreds of years.

Dec is an old Latin word that means **ten: dec**imal / **dec**ade / **dec**athlon

1. **Group the words in the table by their common roots.** *(16 mark*

invention diction spectator dictionary depress inspection spectrum advent

preventative spectacles dictate pressure ventilator express dictator compres

from **dictare**: to say	from **presse**: to press	from **esventer**: to let out	from **specere**: to look

2. **The answers to these definitions share the common root, scope.**

   a A piece of equipment you use to look at the stars. t_____

   b A forecast of a person's future. h_____

   c A piece of equipment that magnifies small objects. m_____

   d A piece of medical equipment used to listen to your chest. st_____

3. **Write two words for each of the common roots below.**

   a phone: _____ _____

   b graph: _____ _____

   c aqua: _____ _____

   d octo: _____ _____

0			24
Tough	OK	Got it!	

Total

/24

Vowel suffixes

The letter strings **ive**, **ic** and **ist** are vowel suffixes and can be added to the end of different words.

expense / expens**ive**   horrify / horrif**ic**   special / special**ist**

If a word **ends** in **e** or **y** the letter must be **removed** before one of these suffixes can be added.

1. **Add the correct suffix to each of these words and write them in the table.**

relate   terrify   balloon

narrate   machine   allergy

expense   photograph   novel

act   artist   mass

acid   conservation   extreme

ive	ic	ist

(15 marks)

2. **Use the new words from question 1 to complete these sentences.**

a Some people are _____ to nuts.

b A person who draws and paints is _____.

c People with a _____ memory remember things easily.

d Some things are very cheap to buy but others are very _____.

e An elephant is a _____ animal.

f A person who writes story books is a _____.

g A _____ is someone to whom you are related.

h Someone who works a machine is a _____.

			Total
0			23
Tough	OK	Got it!	/23

Compound words

Compound words are made by joining **two or three small words** together:

broom + stick = broomstick   crafts + man + ship = craftsmanship

Compound words usually have a **different** meaning from the individual words.

1. **Match the correct pairs and write the compound nouns.**

   a black   cloth   _____   **f** out   night   _____

   b rasp   work   _____   **g** black   room   _____

   c table   bag   _____   **h** good   side   _____

   d hand   berry   _____   **i** moon   bird   _____

   e home   board   _____   **j** cloak   light   _____

2. **Write two compound words that start with each of these words.**

   a bed   _____   _____

   b house   _____   _____

   c any   _____   _____

   d sun   _____   _____

   e some   _____   _____

3. **Make compound words from the list below and complete the sentences.**

   straw   flower   land   news   milk   grass

   hopper   shake   paper   bed   berry   lord

   a Dad likes to read the _____ on Sunday afternoons.

   b I saw a _____ in the small _____ in the garden.

   c "Yakov, can I have a _____ _____ to drink please?"

   d The _____ rented out five houses in the city centre.

0			19
Tough	OK	Got it!	

Total

19 / 19

Diminutives

Diminutives are words that imply a **smaller version** of something. Some are formed by adding **prefixes** or **suffixes** to a root word.

minibus = a small bus   book**let** = a small book   kitchen**ette** = a small kitchen

microcomputer = a small computer   sap**ling** = a small/young tree

Diminutives can also be used as affectionate **abbreviations** for first names, for example **William** is often shortened to **Bill**.

. Add one of the suffixes: let, ling, ten or ock to complete the names of these young animals and birds.

a pig_____   b bull_____   c gos_____

d duck_____   e eag_____   f kit_____

. Complete these words with either the prefix mini or micro.

a _____mal   b _____mum   c _____phone

d _____chip   e _____ature   f _____scope

. Match the full and abbreviated forms of the names below.

a Anthony   Ben   e James   Vicky

b Daniel   Liz   f Timothy   Jim

c Benjamin   Dan   g Nicholas   Tim

d Elizabeth   Tony   h Victoria   Nick

4. Complete each sentence with a word ending with the suffix in brackets.

a I have blonde hair but my sister is a br_____. (ette)

b I wear a silver a_____ around my ankle. (let)

c A du_____ is made from suet and is usually put in beef stew. (ling)

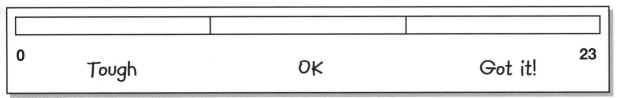

0   Tough   OK   Got it!   23

Total

23

49

Verb endings

Verb endings can **change** depending on:

- which **tense** is used (past, present or future)
- if a verb is put with **another verb** (to be): "I **am going** dancing."

The **first verb changes** but the second verb does not change.

1. **Complete this table using parts of the verb 'to be'.** (4 mark

Person	Past	Present	Future
I	was	am	will
you			
he, she or it		is	
we			
they			will

2. **Write the future tense of these verbs.**

   a to walk: I _____

   b to pack: he _____

   c to run: we _____

   d to swim: they _____

3. **Complete the sentences with the forms of the verbs and tenses shown in brackets.**

   a We _____ Grandma's house at 3 o'clock. (to leave / past tense)

   b My family _____ to the Lake District on Sunday. (to drive / past tense)

   c We _____ house in the Spring. (to move / future tense)

   d I _____ my homework after dinner. (to finish / future)

   e It _____ our Sports Day next Wednesday. (to be / future tense)

   f Our cousins _____ two days ago. (to arrive / past tense)

0	Tough	OK	Got it!	14

Total

14

Comparative endings

> **Comparative endings** are used to compare one thing with another.
>
> John is small. John is small**er** than Asad. Tom is the small**est**.
>
> These suffixes are added to:
> - **adjectives** with **one syllable**.   kind / kind**er**
> - **two-syllable** words that end in **y**. noisy / nois**iest**.
>
> The words **more** or **most** are written **before** adjectives with **two or more** syllables.
>
> This way is **more** practical.   It was the **most** fantastic afternoon.
>
> To add extra emphasis, the word **much** can be used:
>
> John is **much smaller** than Asad. This way is **much more** practical.

1. Change these adjectives into comparisons by adding the suffixes 'er' and 'est'.

a safe _____ _____

b big _____ _____

c pretty _____ _____

> QUICK TIP!
> - **y** becomes **i**
> - wet/wetter
> - drop the **e**
>   larg**e**/larg**er**

2. Choose either more or most to complete these sentences.

a That is the _____ wonderful idea for a present!

b It was _____ interesting than the trip yesterday afternoon.

c "That game is _____ fun than some, but this game is the _____ fun."

3. Complete the sentences, adding extra emphasis where possible.

a Her top is _____ expensive than mine but Al's is the __dearest__.

b My brother thinks he is _____ intelligent than me.

c Julie said that the twins could not be _____ different!

d It was the _____ colourful fabric – _____ better than the other one!

0		10
Tough	OK	Got it!

Total

/10

Plural nouns

Many nouns are made into **plurals** by just adding **s** or **es**:

　　book / book**s**　　bus / bus**es**　　　　wish / wish**es**　　　computer / computer**s**

For those that end in

- a **vowel** and **y**, add **s**: da**y** / day**s**
- a **consonant** and **y**, change the **y** to **i** and add **es**: pop**py** / popp**ies**
- **o** either add **s** or **es**: rati**o** / ratio**s**　　　grott**o** / grott**oes**.

Some nouns do not follow the rules. They have irregular plurals: cris**is** / cris**es**.

The singular and plural of some nouns is the same: **scissors**.

1. **Write the plural form of these nouns.**

   a calendar _____　　b coach _____　　c kiss _____

   d domino _____　　e fox _____　　f holiday _____

   g photo _____　　h cry _____　　i accident _____

   j glass _____　　k gas _____　　l watch _____

2. **Circle the correct irregular plural forms of these singular nouns.**

   a cactus　cactuses / cacti / cactus　　b oasis　oases / oasises / oasi

   c antenna antennae / antennas / anti　d gateau　gateaus / gateaux / gatus

   e fungus　funguses / fungus / fungi　　f formula formulae / formulas / formi

3. **Circle the incorrect plurals and write the correct spellings.**

   a There are many specieses of butterfly. _____

   b We saw twenty sheeps in the field and five deers. _____ _____

   c I caught three salmons and five trouts for the dinner party. _____ _____

   d Two new serieses were advertised on the television. _____

0			22	Total
Tough	OK	Got it!		/22

Connectives

A **connective** is a **word or phrase** that **links clauses and sentences.**

- **Conjunctions** join ideas (clauses) within a sentence.
  I was upset **but** I didn't say anything.

- **Connecting adverbs** link ideas (clauses) but they remain separate sentences.
  I was upset. **However**, I didn't say anything.

---

1. Circle the connectives in these sentences.

a Mum said that if I finished my homework then I could watch television.

b He went to the High Street, although he needed to be back home.

c It was a horrible day so I decided to stay at home.

d It was too dangerous to go swimming due to the strong winds.

e She was worn out but eventually she got to bed.

2. Choose a connective from the list to complete these sentences.

nevertheless   in fact   whereas   however   as a result

unless   therefore   on the other hand   since

a He thought he was late, _____, he was early.

b "The solution, _____, is to revise as often as possible!"

c "You won't be able to go on the trip _____ a space becomes free."

d She thought Carrie was right. _____, David also had a point.

e His one concern, _____, was how to be in two places at the same time.

f The school was improving; _____, they had a party at the end of term.

g Pete was injured; _____, the team continued to play the game.

h "I haven't watched TV much _____ I started reading this book."

i Jo liked playing football, _____ Merlinda preferred athletics.

0	Tough	OK	Got it! 14

Total

/14

53

Different kinds of sentences

The **structure** of a sentence changes when the **sentence type** changes.

I shall cut the hedge. = a **positive statement** saying what you plan to do.

Shall I cut the hedge? = a **question** asking if you can do something.

Cut the hedge! = an **order** telling someone to do something.

I shall not cut the hedge. = a **negative statement** saying what you won't do.

1. **What type of sentences are these?**

   a Where are we going? _____

   b I am playing football after school. _____

   c Shall we go to the park this afternoon? _____

   d Put me down! _____

   e I won't go out tonight. _____

> **QUICK TIP!**
> Remember, punctuation changes when sentence types change.

2. **Change these statements into orders.**

Positive statement	Order
a I will come with you.	
b I shall sit down.	
c I will never do it again.	
d I'd like you to leave.	

3. **Change these sentences into negative statements.**

   a I'm staying with Neha tonight. _____

   b We are going shopping now. _____

   c I can do my homework later. _____

0			12
Tough	OK	Got it!	

Total

/12

Colons and semicolons

> A **colon** (:) **introduces** words, phrases, sentences, quotations or lists.
>
> The inscription read**:** 'To Maggie, love Kabir'
>
> **Semicolons** (;) have two jobs:
>
> - they **join two complete sentences** together:
>
>   Paul is a good pupil**;** he does all his homework.
>
> - they can be used instead of commas in **complex lists**:
>
>   The ingredients included: minced beef**;** canned kidney beans, strained**;** salt and pepper**;** chilli powder and chopped tomatoes.

QUICK TIP!
Never use more than one colon in a sentence.

1. Write in the missing colons in these sentences.

a Some poems have the name of a person as the first line Solomon Grundy.

b The number sequence was as follows two, four, six, eight.

c Alan read the quotation aloud To be or not to be!

2. Write in the missing semicolons in these sentences.

a She felt dizzy in the sun it was a very hot day.

b He liked his new bike it was great to ride.

c I need: a large, firm cucumber four fresh river salmon and a box of grapes.

3. Write in the missing colons and semicolons in these sentences.

a The speech began with these words "Friends, Romans, countrymen!"

b We were having a stir-fry for dinner Mum had to keep stirring the food.

c Our new car has many features air-conditioning all electric windows two airbags in the front a CD player and central locking.

0			9
Tough	OK	Got it!	

Total

9

Hyphens

> **Hyphens join words together.**
>
> They can:
> - make one word out of two (or more) words: **mother-in-law   part-time**
> - join numbers: **forty-six   ninety-three**
> - avoid confusion: **re-sign** the note (instead of 'resign from a job')
> - separate some prefixes from root words: **ex-teacher   non-stick**.

1. **Rewrite these sentences putting the hyphens in the right places.**

   a They-went to Bourton on the Water-for a wonderful day-out.

   _____

   b He-took his three year old-sister to the park-during half time.

   _____

   c The decision making-process was easy; it had to be a four wheel drive-car.

   _____

   _____

2. **Write in the missing hyphens in these sentences.**

   a Mr James is Steve's father in law and Susie is his sister in law.

   b They had a second hand three piece suite in the lounge.

   c Sixty three people went to the private party which was a low key event.

   d Jon was clean shaven for his interview and brimming with self confidence.

   e Marie decided to re cover the chair and then re place it in the dining room.

   f A passer by saw the break in and called the police.

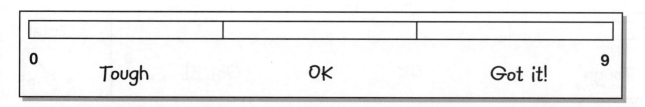

Total

0   9

Tough   OK   Got it!

9

56

Dashes

> A **single dash**:
> - attaches an **extra point** to a sentence: She thought it was shut – but was it?
> - introduces information that **explains more** about the previous sentence:
>   She won't be in today – she is not well.
>
> A **pair of dashes**:
> - separate non-essential information in a sentence:
>   Our last house – the one in the country – had a large garden.

Rewrite these sentences with the dashes in the correct positions.

a It was a once in a lifetime – opportunity and they took it.

_____

b We had a fantastic time – at the theme park everyone had a lot of fun.

_____

c Due to – recent events see the attached note the car park – is now closed.

_____

d He had lost – the map the map which showed the location of the treasure.

_____

2. Write in the missing dashes in the correct positions.

a The girls Ellen and Adhira were going swimming after school.

b We slept in the car for the night very uncomfortable!

c "That's a great place to visit do you have anywhere else in mind?"

d He wanted to go but could he?

e They were looking for the diary the diary that held all the answers.

f Lee has a little brother he likes to tease him a lot.

			Total
0 Tough	OK	Got it! 10	/10

Poetry

Read this poem, then answer the questions.

The deer

They stood there at the field's edge, like swimmers
too nervous to go in. They kicked up their heels
daintily – dancers practising their steps –
and their ears flickered to and fro,
to and fro, listening
for a dog or a man.

Their spring coats were glossy
as the new grass, soft as wool
that you wanted to stroke.
and I almost could. I was down-wind,
hidden by the oaks. I got that close
before they turned
and saw me and were gone,
moving like water down the hillside
in a stream of brown.

1. **Where are the deer standing at the start of the poem?**

   _____

2. **How do we know that the deer are very shy?**

   _____

3. **What other sign do the deer give that they are looking out for danger?**

   _____

4. **What two things were they particularly frightened of?**

   _____

5. **What adverb tells us how the deer moved their feet?**

   _____

What time of year is it?

_____

What were the coats of the deer like, and what colour were they?

_____

_____

What were the reasons that the poet could get close to the deer?

_____

Why was being 'down-wind' important?

_____

0. Write down all the similes and metaphors in the poem in two groups.

   a Similes _____

_____

   b Metaphors _____

_____

1. What tells you that the poet finds the deer beautiful?

_____

_____

_____

0	Tough	OK	Got it!	12

Total

/ 12

Persuasive writing

The aim of **persuasive writing** is to try and convince the reader to share the writer point of view. Persuasive writing can be found in: **opinion pieces** in magazines; **letters of request**, **protest** or **complaint**; and **advertisements**.

The key features of persuasive writing are:

clear, structured paragraphs

emotive language

repetition of key words or phrases

stating opinion as fact

alliteration ('**b**ags of **b**eans')

metaphors and similes

powerful verbs and adjectives

exaggeration

Read this magazine article then answer the questions.

1. **What is this article about? Circle the correct answer.**

   a foxes

   b food

   c litter

2. **What could happen if you offend? Circle the correct answer.**

   a you could be fined

   b you could be taken to court

   c both of these

Lazy LITTER Louts!

LITTER is a health hazard – a ticking time bomb! It encourages maggots, flies, rats and foxes, all of which spread serious diseases.

But how does this LITTER find its way into our environment? It doesn't create itself! LITTER is discarded by thoughtless individuals who drop it where they stand, toss it out of car windows or dump it in bagfuls in public places. And what do we mean by LITTER?

Dropped food or scraps; empty food packaging; sweet wrappers; empty bottles and cans; waste paper; unwanted chewing gum – these are all examples of LITTER.

So how can YOU make sure you're not the culprit? Take your LITTER home with YOU or put it in a dustbin.

Discarding LITTER is an offence which carries an on-the-spot fine of £50, or more if the case goes to court.

Make sure YOU are not a LITTER-BUG!

3. **List all the different types of litter mentioned in the article.** (3 marks, $\frac{1}{2}$ mark for each)

_____

_____

What is a litter-bug? _____

Find three examples of alliteration in the text.   (3 marks)

_____

_____

What metaphor is used to describe litter? _____

What five-word phrase clearly states the main argument of the writer?

_____

Do you think the writer exaggerates the dangers of litter? If so how?

_____

_____

_____

Which four powerful verbs are used to describe how litter is created?

_____

0. Why do you think the word litter is repeated so often in capitals?

_____

_____

1. The article tries to frighten people about the dangers of litters in two ways.
   What are they?   (2 marks)

   a _____

   b _____

Tough	OK	Got it!

0   16

Total

/ 16

How am I doing?

1. **Write the correct spellings for these wa and wo words.**

   a toosum _____   **b** wosp _____   **c** wurry _____

   d woarta _____   **e** soard _____   **f** sworm _____

2. **Group these ou and ough words together by their pronunciations.**   *(5 mar*

   tough   hour   bought   your   rough   nought   enough

   shout   bough   through   boulder   though   mould   you   route

oh	ow	oo	uh	aw

3. **Write three words for the common root below.**

   dec _____   _____   _____

4. **Add the suffixes ive, ic or ist to these words.**

   a relate_____   **b** narrate_____

   c allergy_____   **d** terror_____

   e novel_____   **f** photograph_____

5. **Join the compound words and put them in the sentences.**

   shoe   house   **a** Mum put her sandals in a _____ .

   play   box   **b** Our _____ at school is huge.

   club   ground   **c** We kept the cricket equipment in the _____

6. **Complete these diminutives by adding the correct prefix or suffix.**

   a duck_____   **b** _____ature   **c** owl_____   **d** kitchen_____

Complete the sentences using words with comparative endings or the words more or most.

a Ahmed could run _____ than Sylvan.

b Her coat is _____ expensive than mine but Sal's is the cheap_____.

c It was the _____ fantastic afternoon!

Circle the correct plural forms for these nouns.

a spade   spadae / spedes / spades   b fungus   fungus / fungi / funguses

c library   libraries / librarys / librarees   d sock   socks / sox / sockes

Choose one of these connectives to complete these sentences.

however   if ... then   no matter how

a It was late, _____ it was important that the work was finished.

b Mum said that _____ they tidied up _____ they could watch television.

c It was not easy to get things right, _____ hard they tried.

0. What sentence types are these: order, question or statement?

a "I'd like to go home now," said Dad. _____

b "Where are we going Mum?" _____

c "Go to your room at once!" _____

11. Put the missing colons and semicolons into these sentences.

a Here is the combination for the safe two, four, six, eight.

b Juliet said these words "A rose by any other name".

c The recipe needed four fresh apples small green grapes and cherries.

12. Put the missing hyphens and dashes into these sentences.

a My aunt lives in Moreton in Marsh.

b He thought it was going to be amazing and it was!

c He saw his ex teacher at the supermarket and hid!

Total

44

Try the 9–10 years book

Vowel endings

> Many nouns that end with a vowel end in **e**:
>   tun**e**
> Some nouns end with **a i o** or **u**:
>   camer**a**   scamp**i**   her**o**   gn**u**

1. **Use a vowel to complete these nouns to do with food and music.**

   a banj_   **b** pizz_   **c** risott_   **d** raviol_   **e** banan_   **f** concert_

   g cell_   **h** past_   **i** viol_   **j** pian_   **k** disc_   **l** bong_

2. **Write the names of the animals described. They all end with a vowel.**

   a A striped animal with hooves that lives in Africa.   z_____

   b An Australian animal that keeps its young in a pouch.   k_____

   c A dangerous, hooded snake that lives in Africa and India. c_____

> To change a word ending in a vowel from singular to plural follow these rules.
> If the noun ends in:
> • **one vowel** add **s** or **es**   camer**a** / camera**s**   her**o** / hero**es**
> It's hard sometimes to know if the plural is **s** or **es**!
> • **two vowels** add **s**   tatt**oo** / tatto **os**

> **QUICK TIP!**
> The singular and plural of some words are the same.

3. **Write the plural of these words.**

   a igloo _____   **b** piano_____   **c** echo_____

   d cargo_____   **e** mango_____   **f** case_____

4. **Complete the sentences by changing the nouns in brackets to plurals.**

   a Mum put _____ and _____ in the salad. (tomato / avocado)

   b The cowboys swirled their _____ around their heads. (lasso)

   c Mum uses _____ to make chips. (potato)

0			24
Tough	OK	Got it!	

Total
/24